250 Mini Tongue Twisters

World Knowledge

ISBN-13: 9781973132479

1) The blue bird looked bigger than Bob's black bird.

2) Carla was cooking cabbage for Carl and Kenny.

3) Dance delightfully until dawn then dance again.

4) Adam ate the apples that he got in Appletown.

5) She saw sixty ships sailing in the salty sea.

6) Don't wish too many wishes on Wednesday.

7) She thought the seal was short and stocky.

8) I wish I had a wish for every day I wished.

9) Tim thought the truck was

terrific and tall.

10) The cat caught Candy eating candy with Kevin.

11) Eve and Earl were outside in the evening.

12) You can't see what Yvonne can see.

13) Carl's cook eats too many cookies when cooking.

14) Betty began the day before she thought she would begin.

15) Peter solved a problem for Paul and Priscilla.

16) Fly to the trees and see what you can see.

17) Faith thought leaning French was fancy.

18) Everything was too tiny for little Tim to try on.

19) Bob went on a boat to Brad's house in Breeboat.

20) Joe could joke around and tell many good jokes.

21) Several sailors saw six swimming swans in many seas.

22) Sit outside and sing silly songs with Sal.

23) Cheryl saw a cup of coffee in the copper coffee cup.

24) Measure the mushy mushrooms for Mark's mixture.

25) Six soldiers saw seven swans swimming near sixteen soldiers.

26) Ted saw thirty tan tires lined

up near the tall tower.

27) Frank and Faith ordered fried fish because it was Friday.

28) Mommy made many muffins on Monday morning in Muffinbrook.

29) Write the right words down when you are writing.

30) Barbara's bird was bigger than Brad's big bird.

31) Smile until you smile until next summer.

32) Tom's twelve tires were all tied up.

33) Sam solved the science problem with Sally and Steve.

34) She said she saw what Steve

saw on Saturday.

35) Clap your hands and clap them with Cleo.

36) Kim's cold kitchen was cleaner than Kenny's cold kitchen.

37) Larry's lawn was large and full of little lemons.

38) Bob bought a basket full of blue balls and black bats.

39) Teresa threw three balls in the tall trees in Townbrook.

40) She saw six shells and six sheep near the shore.

41) Peter had purple pickles at Patty's party.

42) Luke likes lakes and little lemons.

43) Steven said it was always sunny in Seabrook and Seastream.

44) The blue bricks were brittle and broken.

45) Sailing sounded simple to Sandy and Sally.

46) Carla saw clowns clowning around at the circus.

47) Brad's block had many big buildings of broken bricks.

48) Papa had a peach and a pear at the party.

49) Crackers and cheese is what Cheryl and Chris craved.

50) Bob's butter was too bitter for Bree.

51) Don't do this and don't do that.

52) Make a mark for Mark and Mitch.

53) Peter likes purple pies and purple peas.

54) Sally's sink sounded like seven ships sailing in the sea.

55) Sal was silly and slow and sounded sleepy.

56) The markers made many dark marks in the dark.

57) The butter was more bitter when Bobby bought it.

58) Wish again before you run out of wishes.

59) Gavin wants to learn Greek in Greece.

60) The turtle was tired from

looking at the tall trees in town.

61) A black bear was near a black bug.

62) Peter packed a bag full of purple peppers.

63) Charlie and Chris like corn and cabbage.

64) Faith counted to five before she counted to fifty.

65) Learning English was easy for Edward in England.

66) Wanda wished the wish that Wendy wished.

67) The problem was simply solved by a simple solution.

68) Sam’s sink was soiled and smelly.

69) Nina needed money to visit Ned in Nedtown.

70) Sal seldom sells shells in the summer.

71) The duck didn't do what David thought it would do.

72) The silver ship never sank in the shiny sea.

73) Try to take the test on Tuesday instead of Thursday.

74) Don's dog didn't know about David's dog.

75) Steve said the seven simple steps were not so simple.

76) The fresh fruit was not fresh enough for Fred and Faith.

77) Betty bought butter for Bobby's

bagel.

78) Three tan balls were thrown from tan trees.

79) Practice makes Percy perfect if he gets enough practice.

80) Margaret made many more of what Mike already made.

81) Mark was mumbling about the mayonnaise on the meat.

82) Dad thought the day was too dark to see a deer in the dark.

83) Nina saw nine nurses in Nursebrook.

84) Try to take the tough test tomorrow with Teddy.

85) The king came to see Carl and Kim in Kingville.

86) Wish for more wishes and then wish for another wish.

87) The cat went camping with Carl and Kim.

88) Ray ran to the river and then the red tree.

89) The cows caught Carl carrying a carton.

90) Jim saw Jay jumping up and down at the gym.

91) The camel saw Carla eating caramel candy.

92) Donna thought David was going to do what Diana did.

93) The gold clowns had gold crowns on their teeth.

94) Rose saw a red bush and then a

redder bush.

95) Throw three balls and then throw thirteen.

96) This summer was the best summer because it was the longest summer.

97) The glass looked greener than the grass looked through the glass.

98) Sit and sit again until you sit on Sunday.

99) Seven silly swimmers were swimming in the sea.

100) Frank's frog looked funny when trying to fly.

101) Roberta ran faster than Richard ever ran in Racebrook.

102) The giraffe saw Gabe near the

gold gate.

103) Mark's mother made muffins for Mandy and Mitch.

104) Jill jumped until she jumped with Jake.

105) The tongue twister twisted Taylor's tongue.

106) Peter said he saw purple people in Purpleville.

107) Karl was from Korea and knew Korean.

108) Only wish for wishes during the week.

109) She saw six sticks and then saw sixteen sticks.

110) Sandy said she saw Sam and Samantha near the sea.

111) Softly say the sounds of the six sentences.

112) Mommy made mushrooms and meatballs on Monday.

113) Tim told Tom tongue twisters about twirling.

114) Kate's cat liked the clean carpet and clean couch.

115) The silly sounds were said by Samantha.

116) Brad bought bitter butter for Brady.

117) The stump was too tall for Stan and Stewart.

118) Fred said his feet were bigger than Frank's feet.

119) April is when April always

visits Adam.

120) Mark wants to go on a mission to the Moon and Mars.

121) Six ships sent signals to six sheep on the sand.

122) Cleo clapped his hands until he clapped with Kate.

123) Don't brush your hair with too many big brushes.

124) Marsha made a mushy mix of mushrooms.

125) The breeze was blowing bigger than the last breeze.

126) Fred's frozen food was fresh and fancy.

127) Sing the silly songs until the songs aren't silly.

128) Vivian likes violets and violet violins.

129) Sally saw seven silly socks near Sal.

130) Sit down then stand before sitting and standing again.

131) Bring the blue boxes to the black boxes.

132) Do this and do that and do this again.

133) Sal sat in a shop that sells snakes.

134) Practice makes perfect when you practice with Patricia.

135) Edith ate eggplant at eight in the evening.

136) Harry had a hard time hearing

Hank.

137) Wilma wishes for windy weather in Windwish.

138) Seven shoes were full of sand and slime.

139) Tell the tongue twister to Tom and Timothy.

140) The fog was frequent in Frogbrook.

141) Matt's mice like merry music.

142) Tom tied his torn tie on Tuesday.

143) Blake saw baked beans in the black basket.

144) Ted was twisting and turning while talking to Teddy.

145) The soap was soapy when Cindy used the soap.

146) Colton can’t cook anything that requires a cook.

147) The street was sandy and slippery for Cindy.

148) Paul poured Patrica’s pudding on the plate.

149) David’s doctor drove from Docville to Doctown.

150) Can they make a better can than the cans from Canton?

151) Sal’s cat slid in the snow when it was snowing.

152) The purple paper was more purple than Paula’s purple paper.

153) Guide the goat near the gate to

Goatville.

154) Tom told Tammy the tough tongue twister that Tommy told Tim.

155) Read that tongue twister that Tom told Teresa.

156) Peter had pipes that were leaking in Paul's place.

157) The horse was happy to see Harry and Henry.

158) Nina knows how to pronounce the nine nouns.

159) The fly saw another fly as he flew on by.

160) Sandy said six silly sounds to Sean.

161) Program the program to be a

perfect program.

162) Eight elephants tried to jump each evening.

163) Six sisters sold several sandy shoes.

164) Floyd's flag was flying near Faith's flowers.

165) Brad fell on his back because of the black bat.

166) Sell all the shoes and sell them swiftly.

167) Bobby saw a black cat and a beautiful bird.

168) The giraffe saw a giant goat in Giraffetown.

169) Bob bought blue balloons for Betty and Barbara.

170) Tim threw three throws at Tom's game.

171) The sailor went to see what was in the sea.

172) Tom's tree was tall and terrific.

173) Slide to the side and slide slowly.

174) The fish were friendly to Fred's friendly fish.

175) Paula practices until she is perfect.

176) Twist and turn until you turn again.

177) Mark made a lot of money from magic motorcycles.

178) The dog didn't know what

Don's dog did.

179) The black and blue bat was big enough to hit the black and blue balls.

180) Lenny had a longer leg than the other leg.

181) Sandy sat on a swing and sang songs to Sheila.

182) Say the small words slowly and silently.

183) Greg greeted Gregory at the gate that looked golden.

184) Wash the windows in the wind for Wendy and Wallace.

185) Sheila said she was shorter than Sally.

186) Betty is the best at building

big bridges.

187) Frank counted to five for five friends.

188) Fred was friendly and from Friendville.

189) Mitch said it was his mission to go to Mars on Monday.

190) George saw a goat near the golden grapes.

191) The smelly sock was in a sink of suds.

192) The clowns were clumsy and couldn’t cook.

193) Fog was in Fogbrook and Fogville.

194) Sal and Sara were sitting on the sink.

195) The salad was salty and sour.

196) Peter and Patricia worked on purple pipes.

197) The black bear had a black hat on a black rack.

198) Several squirrels slid slowly in the snow.

199) Sheila made a choice to choose the cheddar cheese.

200) The tongue twisters seemed twisty and tough.

201) Say all the sounds slowly to Sam.

202) The duck saw the deer near Don's door.

203) The can of candy was near a can that was next to a can of corn.

204) Think of a thought and then think of many thoughts.

205) Several shops sold silly sweaters and silly shoes.

206) Charlie chews celery slowly.

207) The black bike had black brakes and blue bells.

208) Sharply say the sounds in the sentence.

209) The zebra saw a zoo in the shape of a zebra.

210) Samantha's sister sells shoes and sandals.

211) Five fresh fish were served in Fishtown.

212) Kay had a cute kitten that was from Kittenbrook.

213) She said she saw Shelton talking to Sheila.

214) Edward was eating eggs every evening.

215) Seth's sister sells shoes made for sheep.

216) The kitty was near the cotton in the kitchen.

217) Don't sell too many slimy shells near the shore.

218) The silly shark was swimming in the salty sea.

219) The timid tiger was near Tom and Timothy.

220) She was sitting next to six sticky sticks.

221) Sam said sixteen sounds for

Shirley.

222) Surely she saw Samantha swimming.

223) Sal and Sara were sitting on slimy sand.

224) Bring the broken board back to the broken box.

225) Which way is the way to Waterway?

226) The rolling road was full of red rocks.

227) The silly songs were simple to sing.

228) Will was weary when he awoke on Wednesday.

229) Chris likes more cheese on crackers than Carlton likes.

230) Wish for another wish after you wish for one wish.

231) Count with Candy to get more cake and candy.

232) The purple park was perfect for Priscilla and Patty.

233) The camel couldn't climb on Carl's carton.

234) She solved a problem from Sal's list of problems.

235) Gabe likes grapes and gooey candy.

236) The tongue twisters were too tough for Timmy.

237) Carl's chickens caught the chicks going to the country.

238) The smelly socks were sold to

Sam and Sean.

239) The dog saw the blue shoes by the seven blue shoes.

240) She saw the pounds of cheese that Chris craved in Cheeseville.

241) Sal's sneakers were covered in sand and snow.

242) Mark likes milk, mayonnaise, and muffins.

243) Paula's pink pots were pretty and just perfect.

244) Sally and Samantha thought the sand was sticky.

245) Eight elephants saw either other elephants eating in the evening.

246) Colton's cows lived in the

country in Cowville.

247) Daddy does the thirty dirty dishes on Thursday.

248) She sells many shells and sells them on Sunday.

249) Tom's tiny toys were like Tim's terrific toys.

250) The puddle was bigger than Paula's ponds.

24585100R00021

Printed in Great Britain
by Amazon